LINDISFARNE CHURCH

ACKNOWLEDGEMENT

ith thanks to Kerr McGee Oil who supported
the publication of this book.

Design: Paul Welti
Typesetting: Peter Howard

ISBN 0 9519529 1 9

Second printing, this edition printed in Italy

# NORTHUMBER
## IN WATERCOLO

Illustrated by DAPHNE HARRISON

Written by JOHN TAYLOR

*I strove with none, for none was worth my strife,*
*Nature I loved, and next to Nature, Art*

WALTER SAVAGE LANDOR

ANSIS PUBLISHING

# CONTENTS

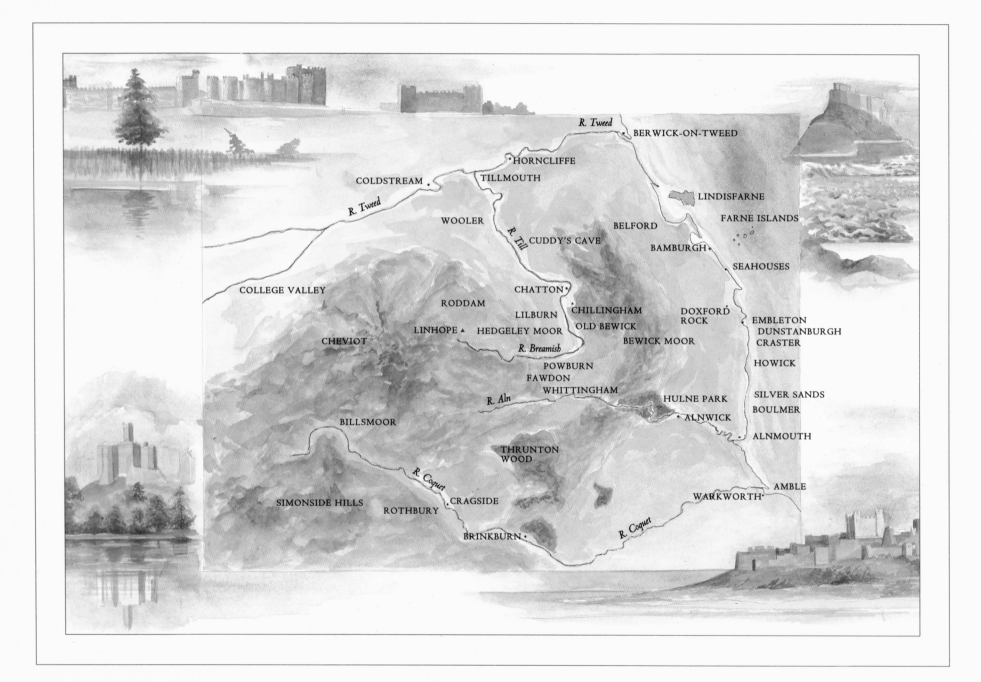

R. Tweed

R. Tweed

BERWICK-ON-TWEED

HORNCLIFFE

COLDSTREAM          TILLMOUTH

LINDISFARNE

WOOLER                    BELFORD          FARNE ISLANDS

R. Till    CUDDY'S CAVE

BAMBURGH

SEAHOUSES

COLLEGE VALLEY                    CHATTON

RODDAM                              CHILLINGHAM          DOXFORD
            LILBURN                                        ROCK        EMBLETON
LINHOPE    HEDGELEY MOOR    OLD BEWICK                              DUNSTANBURGH
CHEVIOT                                                                CRASTER
                    R. Breamish                    BEWICK MOOR

                                                                HOWICK

                              POWBURN
                              FAWDON
                              WHITTINGHAM                              SILVER SANDS

            R. Aln                          HULNE PARK              BOULMER

                                                      ALNWICK

BILLSMOOR                                                            ALNMOUTH

                    THRUNTON
                    WOOD

            R. Coquet                                                    AMBLE

SIMONSIDE HILLS                CRAGSIDE                  WARKWORTH
            ROTHBURY

            BRINKBURN              R. Coquet

# FOREWORD

It has been a great pleasure for me to be involved with this book. Daphne Harrison's exquisite watercolours capture her subjects beautifully, whether they are tiny trout dimpling the surface of a still pool, or windswept castles looming over a bleak shore-line. John Taylor's writing displays a wealth of local knowledge, of history, traditions, legends, and poetry; and it is truly fascinating. I have learnt more about my own "backyard" by reading his commentary, than from living in Northumberland most of my life.

Northumberland is a large county with infinite variety. It is a beautiful and unspoilt land with castles and beaches, purple hills and green valleys, steeped in history and rich in wildlife. This book covers those areas that have most inspired the artist and writer; some well-known landmarks like Lindisfarne and Bamburgh, but also many lesser-known parts, away from the beaten track where breathtaking views, ancient stone markings, or nesting birds have forced Daphne Harrison to reach for her sketch pad. They principally cover the central and northern part of the county — her particular patch.

THE DUKE OF NORTHUMBERLAND

# AUTHOR'S NOTE

In this book, I haven't written much about the birds and other animals, wild-flowers and other plants. It is too great a subject, and there are so many reference books that describe them in more detail than I ever could. Moreover, this book is essentially a show-case for Daphne Harrison's paintings, and whilst places are specific, the flora and fauna are not unique to Northumberland. I have therefore focused on the history of the places depicted in the paintings. Perhaps it would amuse the reader to test his or her knowledge of natural history, by trying to identify the plants and animals in the illustrations, with reference books close at hand.

JOHN TAYLOR

# CHAPTER ONE

# COQUETDALE

*Tho Cheviot's heid is frosty still,*
*He's green below the knee,*
*Sae don yer plaid, and tak yer gad (gaff)*
*An gang awa wi me.*
*Come, busk yer flees, ma auld compeer,*
*We're fudgin an fu fain,*
*We've fushed the Cockett mony a year,*
*An we'll fush her ow're again*

*The Fisher's Garland 1823*

THE NAME "Coquet" – like "Cheviot" – is very old; they are both so old, so pre-historic, that neither is to be found in any of the old written languages that have come down to us; yet, both names are absolutely synonymous with Northumberland.

"Coquetdale" is usually recognised as being the area from Rothbury to Harbottle. Above Harbottle to the Coquet Head is regarded by locals as "Upper Coquetdale". The best time of year to visit Coquetdale is – any time. To those who love it, it always looks fresh and interesting at any time of the day or night, whatever season. August and September time, however, is really hard to beat. The swallows and swifts are gathering on the telephone wires, chattering to each other as they prepare for their long migratory flight far to the south. The heather on the Simonside range is at its purple best, and the bracken has not yet started to die back.

There are many vantage points from which to view the prospect of Coquetdale; from Cartington in the east – just above Thropton; from Whitton – just above Rothbury; from the top of Great Tosson – the highest point in the Simonside hills. A little-used but splendid view point is at the top of Billsmoor, just up from Elsdon and looking east towards Cartington Hill. On the right-hand slope is the Deerpark, and behind it is the purple heather of Darden Edge.

*Coquetdale*

*Cragside*

In days gone by, most of the farmers in the locality had to help maintain the roads in the district as part of their rent. Some supplied stones; some supplied cartage of materials; some of the larger farmers with more staff supplied the labour for ditching and stone-laying. None of them really liked this form of taxation, and some performed their tasks less efficiently than others. An early 18th-century tenant of the Dunns Farm, called Mr Hedley, was a great devotee of card playing and whisky drinking but, it seems, not so diligent in maintaining the Billsmoor road. At a meeting of the local magistrates at Rothbury, Hedley was told by his landlord, Mr Orde of Nunnykirk, to "give more attention" to his responsibilities on Billsmoor road, or he would go to prison. "Ye daurna dee that," Hedley retorted, "the morn's ye'er rent day."

History does not relate whether Hedley went to prison or whether Mr Orde was paid his rent.

Further down, on the floor of the Coquet valley, are the villages of Hepple, Thropton, Snitter and, finally, Rothbury; all based upon ancient Anglian settlements and all close by the river. The river was one of the main reasons for the great Tyneside industrialist and armaments magnate, Sir William (later 1st Lord) Armstrong of Cragside and Bamburgh, deciding to build and develop his great house and estate of Cragside, Rothbury. A keen angler as a boy, and later throughout his manhood, William Armstrong came to Rothbury for holidays, and especially for his fishing. Over a fifty-year period, he purchased in the region of 30,000 acres of neighbouring farms and estates, and planted forests, built farmhouses, cottages, farm steadings and villages — all from the proceeds of his inventive mind and astute business brain. Always uppermost in his mind, there was, as he put it, "the rod and the line, the fly and the fish".

Lord Armstrong died at the turn of the century — active to the last — having built Cragside House, ornamented his estate, and completed the rebuilding of Bamburgh Castle, just to mention a few of his achievements. The story goes that, at his death, he still left over a million pounds in his private, current bank account, equivalent to the purchase price of at least two iron-clad warships or one dreadnought class battle cruiser.

If fishing the Coquet is one great activity – and there are fine runs of sea-trout and salmon in the spring and autumn floods – then poaching is the other. There is still constant warfare waged by both sides on the riverbank; not, however, on the scale that used to occur. In the past, like most other poaching, the illegal taking of fish was "for the pot", not the commercial operation that it has now become. "Lamping" at night (wading with a trident and a strip of flaming tarry rope to attract the fish); "tick-ling" under the river bank with the aid of a handkerchief; or "stroke hauling" with cruel, rake-hooks on a line; or just the simple "gaff" – were all to feed the family or the collie dogs. Modern-day water bailiffs, with the aid of motor vehicles, radios, mobile telephones and night sights, have limited these nefarious activities. As one famous, local poacher puts it, "it's cheaper to buy farmed salmon nowadays".

The river Coquet stretches forty-five miles from Coquet Head to Amble Bay. Almost all of it is in private ownership, with large stretches of it belonging to the Cragside and Northumberland Estates, who lease most of their fishing to local Angling Associations. Most of the Associations' water can be fished on a day-ticket basis at a reasonable cost.

Oh! green lanes of Northumberland,
What Springs have come, all cowslip-drest,
To strew their gems on earth's green breast.

Oh! green lanes of Northumberland,
What Summer winds have paused to play
Through white festoons of hawthorn spray.

Oh! green lanes of Northumberland,
What Autumn nights have touched the flow'rs,
And shut them in the sunset hours.

Oh! white lanes of Northumberland,
What Winter winds have brought the snows
To drift and fill the long hedgerows.

JOHN ROWELL WALKER; "Northumbrian Lanes"

*Lilburn Pond, Glendale*

*Coquetdale*

*Sharperton Village on the Coquet*

*Coquetdale from Billsmoor looking east*

*Simonside Hills*

# CHAPTER TWO

# BRINKBURN PRIORY

BRINKBURN PRIORY was founded in the reign of King Henry I, third son of William the Conqueror. The Priory was dedicated to St Peter by William de Bertram, Baron of Mitford, who put it under the control of the Order of Black Canons of St Augustine.

There is a tradition in Northumberland that in the Middle Ages, Brinkburn – surrounded by dense woodland that concealed it and rendered it all but unapproachable except by river – was frequently and unsuccessfully sought after by Scottish reivers. On one occasion the monks, having seen the Scots leaving the area, waited awhile and then rang the Priory bell in joyful celebration. Alas, the thieving Scots, having lain hidden, heard the bell and, following its chimes, entered the monastery whilst the monks were at prayer. After terrifying the monks and pillaging the holy fabric, they set it on fire and threw the bell into a deep pool of the river Coquet, which lies alongside the Priory.

A branch of the Roman road called Watling Street – or the Devil's Causeway as we know it – crosses the river Coquet a little below Brinkburn Priory. The remains of the piers of the Roman Bridge are sometimes visible when the river level is low, as well as some ashlar work on the north side which is almost covered with tree roots and scrub. On the hill above the priory are traces of an early building, believed to be either Roman or Romano-British, just a few yards from the military way. There are also indications of a rampart and ditch across the neck of land, and foundations of several other buildings on the site.

At the suppression of the religious houses by King Henry VIII, there were ten Canons in residence here and the annual revenue was estimated at £68.19s.10d. In 1550 the Priory and its lands were given to the then Earl of Warwick. Later in that century, it became the property of George Fenwick who was a Commissioner of Enclosures in the Middle Marches and held land at Stanton and Bywell.

*Brinkburn Priory*

Some form of manor house has stood on the site of part of the Priory since the Dissolution of the Monasteries and, through time, became a residence of the Clavering and Fenwick families. The Priory itself remained a ruin until restored in the mid-19th century by a Mr Cadogan using Thomas Austin, the Newcastle architect. The Manor House was improved in the earlier part of that century when John Dobson was involved in some of the restoration work. In 1866, William Armstrong, later Lord Armstrong of Cragside, supported the Priory restoration by donating an altar, the organ and the bell, as part of his early philanthropic work.

The Priory is reputed to have a ghost, which has been witnessed by several people over the years, and buried treasure was found during one of the many restoration projects in the 19th century. It is also believed that parts of the missing bell, thrown in by the Scots, were recovered from the Bell Pool in the Coquet.

# CHAPTER THREE

# WARKWORTH HERMITAGE AND CASTLE

*A little lonely hermitage there stood*
*Down in a dale by a river's side,*
*Beneath a mossy cliff, o'erhung with wood;*
*And in the living rock, there close beside,*
*Wherein the Hermit daily went to say*
*His lonely prayers, each morn and eventide;*
*Thereby the crystal stream did gently play*
*Which through the woody vale came rolling down*

SPENCER

HIGH SUMMER on the River Coquet. The swallows and swifts have completed their long, hazardous journey from the coasts of North Africa to settle near the mouth of one of Northumberland's favourite rivers, building and moulding their nests from the muddy clay of the river banks, under the eaves and lintels of one of the country's best kept secrets, as they have done for centuries.

Warkworth Hermitage was dedicated to the Holy Trinity, and was continuously occupied from its foundation in the fourteenth century until the Dissolution of the Monasteries in the reign of King Henry VIII. Just before this, in 1537, it was listed among the possessions of the Earl of Northumberland:

*Warkworth Castle from the Hermitage*

*Hermytoges. One at Warkeworth, being a very propre Howse buylded oute of a rocke of stone with many commodities thereto belongynge, whereof Sr. George Lancastre preste, being a well benefyced man, ys now incumbent and hath by letters patentes of the foresaid late erle for terme of his lyff a yearly salarye oute of the lordshippe of Warkeworth of XX marcs and pasture for XII kyne and a bull and their folowers and ii horses and XX lodes of wood, and every Sondaye a draught of fysshe.*

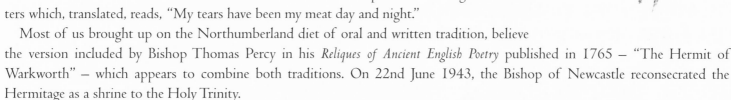

There are two traditions concerning the origin of the Hermitage. On the one hand, it is believed to have been built by a Northumbrian knight, mourning the death of his beloved. The other tradition says the same knight founded it in expiation of the murder of his brother. Whatever the truth of the matter, there is a faded inscription in old English characters which, translated, reads, "My tears have been my meat day and night."

Most of us brought up on the Northumberland diet of oral and written tradition, believe the version included by Bishop Thomas Percy in his *Reliques of Ancient English Poetry* published in 1765 – "The Hermit of Warkworth" – which appears to combine both traditions. On 22nd June 1943, the Bishop of Newcastle reconsecrated the Hermitage as a shrine to the Holy Trinity.

Warkworth Castle dominates the village and the countryside for miles around. A fortress was first recorded here in 737, when Ceolwulf, King of Northumbria, bestowed it on the monks of Lindisfarne. Later this became the site of a Saxon "worth" or palace of the Ocgingas royal family of Bamburgh. On the ruins of this Henry of Huntingdon, son and heir of King David I of Scotland, erected the first motte and bailey fortress in 1140. In 1158, however, following the period of civil strife under Stephen and Matilda, Henry II of England granted Warkworth to Roger Fitz-Richard, whose descendants lost it in the next century for supporting the Baron's cause in the Magna Carta struggle. In 1332 it was granted by Edward III to the second Baron Percy of Alnwick as a reward for the active support that powerful noble had given Edward in his conflicts in Wales and Scotland, as he fought to regain his birthright.

Roger Fitz-Roger, grandson of Roger Fitz-Richard, laid down the present outline of the castle on Henry of Huntingdon's artificial mound, but it is generally accepted that Henry Percy (1368-1409), 1st Earl of Northumberland and father of Hotspur, developed it to its present form, using stone from the old quarry at Birling, just north of the village. Certainly it was the most favoured home of the early Percys.

Apart from the effect of the elements, the present ruinous condition of the castle can be blamed on three men. Sir John Forster of Bamburgh, deputy warden of the Eastern Marches under Lord Hundson, played a major role in destroying the Percy hegemony following the failed rising of the Northern Earls in 1569. He ruthlessly plundered both Alnwick and Warkworth Castles to improve his residences at Alnwick Abbey and Bamburgh Castle, to such an extent that the Lord Warden Hundson, allegedly the illegitimate half-brother of Queen Elizabeth I, was moved to protest strongly to her Secretary of State, William Cecil. His protests were, however, ignored, and in 1603, James I, travelling past Warkworth on his way south to succeed to Elizabeth's throne, "marvelled at the decay of such an important stronghold".

Oliver Cromwell was the second "architect" of Warkworth Castle's destruction. As Lord Protector of the Commonwealth, he ordered the slighting (or rendering indefensible) of this important strategic position, for fear of it being occupied by the Scots, fighting for the Royalist cause of Charles II, or indeed by English Royalists. He then moved north to engage and destroy the Scottish army at the battle of Dunbar in 1650. The 6th Duke of Somerset (the "Proud Duke"), who married the heiress of the 11th Earl of Northumberland, considered rebuilding Warkworth Castle as a principal residence during a period of political adversity and, in fact, did some important refacing work on the Keep; but on regaining political power, turned his attention elsewhere. A bailiff, Joseph Clarke, was the third and final despoiler of the castle. With permission from the Duchess of Somerset, he removed 272 "waynes" or cartloads of stone, lead and timber to build the bailiff's mansion at Chirton, Tynemouth.

Among the legends surrounding Warkworth Castle, there is a tale of hidden treasure. In 1314, Hugh de Cressingham, Lord Treasurer of England to the hapless Edward II, was slain by the Scots at Bannockburn. Part of the treasure placed in his care was

recovered from the battlefield and, by a circuitous route, eventually came to be lodged at Warkworth on its way south. There was some discrepancy between the amount lodged and the amount eventually returned to the Tower of London, but a legal inquiry held by the Exchequer Barons proved inconclusive and it was all put down to the "heat and smoke of war". At a later date the then custodian of the castle is said to have dreamt, on three consecutive nights, of treasure contained in a "yetling" (a cast iron cooking pot) covered by a blue stone, near the castle well; unfortunately, he told a neighbour, and when, after two or three days, he went to inspect the well, he found a recently disturbed blue stone moved from the wall of the well. The end of the story is that the neighbour shortly afterwards became very rich.

Warkworth is a peaceful place these days; the riverbank is quiet except when the tourists boat on the river, visit the castle and picnic on the riverside. Most Saturdays in summertime, the village cricket team entertain their opponents, and sometimes defeat them, replacing the clamour of medieval warfare.

The Hermitage can be approached by boat from the landing place just below the castle, or by footpath from the old bridge at the northern end of the village, along the north bank of Coquet. Also on the north of the river is Hermitage Farm, notable for its tidy husbandry and its delightful farm sign of a border collie. There is some justification for believing that the tofts, which are part of this farm, were originally part of the pasturage for the hermit's animals.

HERMITAGE

# CHAPTER FOUR

# ALNWICK CASTLE

ALNWICK CASTLE is the principal seat of the Duke of Northumberland and the Percy family. Its early history is almost certainly connected with ancient Romano-Britons and Saxons. It was Yvo de Vesci, the first Norman Baron of Alnwick, who erected the earliest parts of the present castle around 1100. In 1309 Sir Henry de Percy became the owner of the Barony of Alnwick, and set about the restoration of the castle with a view to converting it into a stronghold fit to maintain itself in the warfare of the period. The portions of his work which still remain are the semi-circular tower on the north-east side of the Keep, the middle gateway between the Outer and Second Baileys, the Abbot 's Tower, the Western Garret, Auditor's Tower, Eastern Garret, the lower part of the Record Tower and the Postern Tower.

The early Percys maintained Alnwick Castle as a forward base for the centuries of border warfare with Scotland, initiated by Edward I and ending with the Union of the Crowns in 1603. Henry, the 2nd Baron Percy, continued the restoration of the castle which his father had begun. At this period, the garrison consisted of 3 knights, 37 esquires and 40 hobelars (light horsemen) as well as a large number of men-at-arms.

After the Union, the castle fell into decay and, by the late 17th century, it was almost a ruin although it continued to be the residence of the Baronial officials. In the early 18th century, the 6th Duke of Somerset (who married Elizabeth, the Percy heiress) repaired and fitted up a portion of the castle for his residence. His son, the 7th Duke of Somerset, frequently stayed at Alnwick during the reign of George II. He was the first of his family to reside there after an absence of over 100 years. His only daughter, Elizabeth, who was heir to the Barony and the Northumberland estates, married Sir Hugh Smithson, a Yorkshire baronet. In 1750, Smithson reorganised the administration of the estates and introduced up-to-date methods of farming, equipment and management; he also planted large areas with trees. In a few years, by his business capacity, energy and enterprise, he transformed the appearance of the countryside around Alnwick. In 1755, Smithson and his wife commenced the rebuilding of Alnwick Castle. The architect was the celebrated Robert Adam, who adopted the style generally known as "Gingerbread" or "Strawberry Hill" Gothick.

*Alnwick Castle*

*The pond, Rock Village*

*Alnwick Castle*

Sir Hugh Smithson, who was reputed to be the most handsome man in England at the time, was a close friend and supporter of King George III, serving him in 1763 as Lord Lieutenant of Ireland. George III created Smithson Earl, and later Duke of Northumberland (1763). An amusing anecdote of the time relates that the new Duke suggested to the King that he was the only Northumberland never to have received the Order of the Garter, to which the King replied that "only a Smithson would *ask* for the Garter", implying that a Percy would not. The Duke's children took the Percy name which has remained with their descendants ever since.

Algernon, 4th Duke of Northumberland, served in the Navy during the Napoleonic wars and retired with the rank of Admiral. He travelled extensively in Africa and the near East, and was a liberal patron of the arts and sciences, especially archaeology. He rebuilt most of the farmhouses and cottages on his estate and, when this work was finished, he set about another complete restoration of Alnwick Castle. The work was begun in 1855 under the direction of Salvin, whilst the interior decoration was entrusted to a celebrated Italian architect and archaeologist, Canina. Much of what is now seen of Alnwick Castle was done during this restoration. The 4th Duke died in 1865, without enjoying the full splendour of the work he had instigated, which was completed during the lifetime of the 6th Duke.

*River Aln below Hulne Abbey*

# CHAPTER FIVE

# HULNE PARK

## BRIZLEE TOWER

Set within Hulne Park, on the summit of Brizlee Hill, is the elegant and unusual Brizlee Tower. Built by the 1st Duke of Northumberland as a viewpoint, the original model for it was reputed to have been a bit of French patisserie. The Duke was so pleased with the ingenious design of the cake placed before him, that he ordered an exact copy to be built in the form of a tower. This was executed by Mathew Mills, mason of Alnwick. On the Tower are several medallions and inscriptions in Latin, which translate: "Look about you. I have measured out all these things; they are by orders, it is my planning; many of these trees have even been planted by my hand. Hugh, 1st Duke." The tower is 66 feet high with a balcony around it and, at the very top, a curious iron grate which was to be used as a beacon in the Napoleonic Wars. This raises the height to over 90 feet. To the west of the tower there are spectacular views of Whittingham Vale and the Cheviots and, on a clear day, Flodden Field. The prospect to the east is of the coastal plain of Northumberland from the mouth of the river Coquet north to the Farne Islands.

## THE LONG STONE

Near to the tower is an ancient stone obelisk, known as the "Long Stone". There is no recorded history of how this came to be here. It is certainly mentioned in early medieval charters but with no reason given for its existence. It may have been an ancient boundary mark, or perhaps it is connected with the mysterious prehistoric cup-and-ring markings in the area (see p.75). It is a remarkable viewing point and, at the right time of day, has a most magnificent prospect. Thirteen castles are reputed to be visible from it: Dunstanburgh, Bamburgh, Ford, Lindisfarne, Coupland, Barmoor, Callaly, Alnwick, Warkworth, Cartington, and Chillingham in Northumberland, Ayton in Berwickshire and Hume in Roxburghshire.

*Brizlee Tower and the Long Stone, Hulne Park*

## MONK'S CAVE

On the north side of Brizlee Hill is an ancient sandstone cave, watched over by its sentinel. The cave is generally believed to have been the home of Ralph Fresborn, a Northumbrian crusader, who, on his return from the Holy Land, is reputed to have lived as a hermit here. The cave used to be known as "The Nine Years Aud Cave" but there is no written record as to why it was so called. The sentinel – a monument to the hermit – is believed to have been carved by the same school of stonemasons who renewed many of the statues on the walls of Alnwick Castle in the mid-19th century.

## HULNE ABBEY

Ralph Fresborn was a colleague of William de Vesci with whom, on their return from the crusades, he founded Hulne Abbey in about 1240 for the Carmelite order of friars. This was a smaller order than the Premonstratensians (White Friars) who occupied Alnwick Abbey for centuries. Within the Abbey, there is a delightful gothick tower built by the 1st Duke and Duchess of Northumberland and designed by Robert Adam. The remains of the ancient church, with its vestry and refectory, are still there. The Gatehouse and the walls are in a better state of presentation.

## ALNWICK ABBEY

The gatehouse is the only remaining part of the great Abbey of Alnwick, which was one of the richest and most important in Northumberland. The White Friars, with their vast wealth, were continually feuding with the poverty-stricken Carmelite Friars at neighbouring Hulne Abbey, over matters of religious precedence and landownership. During the Border Wars, the Abbot of Alnwick Abbey had the use of the Abbot's Tower in Alnwick Castle as a place of refuge. At the Dissolution of the Monasteries, the Abbey became the home of the rascally Sir John Forster, deputy Warden of the Eastern Marches, who pillaged Alnwick Castle and other nearby properties and used the materials to enhance the Abbey and his Castle of Bamburgh. After the Crown sold these ecclesiastical properties in the early 17th century, they were lived in by a variety of families before coming into the ownership of the Percy family in the middle of the 19th century, when Hulne Park was finally enclosed by its great wall.

*Alnwick Abbey and the Monk's Cave*

[ 33 ]

*Hulne Abbey*

*From Heckley, looking towards Hulne Park*

# CHAPTER SIX

# HOWICK

HOWICK IS famous as the home of the 2nd Earl Grey of "Reform Bill" fame, who inherited it from his uncle, Sir Henry Grey, in 1801, and made it his lifetime home. It is also famous for its arboretum which contains many unusual, fine and mature specimen trees and shrubs. Although this arboretum has been long established, there has been much new planting in recent years, with some specimens grown from seed collected from all over the world. The public are admitted to the grounds of the Hall, which are well worth a visit, especially in spring time when the daffodils abound. "The Long Walk" is particularly attractive, a private pathway leading from the Hall to the Church of St Michael. The present Howick Hall was rebuilt after a terrible fire in 1928, which gutted the previous house built by Sir Henry Grey.

The cliffs along the coast here contain some wonderful examples of the geology of the district, showing formations of limestone, shale and whinstone, particularly if standing opposite Howick village on the cliffs looking north towards Cullernose Point at Craster. There are plenty of fossils present in the rocks and cliffs of the shoreline. Near to Howick Seahouses, there is evidence, at very low tide, of the remains of a prehistoric, petrified forest exposed by the repeated action of winter storms.

The country around Horwick is very good agricultural land, but it overlies minerals which have been "cropped" extensively over the centuries. Most of the land lies on the limestone which, in turn, overlies the great "whin-sill" at varying depths. Shallow outcrops of coal were mined in this area and limestone was excavated extensively for use in the agricultural improvements in the 17th and 18th centuries. Latterly, it is the whinstone which has been quarried on a large scale. This is of particularly fine quality and is used in the manufacture of concrete pipes and roadmaking aggregates.

*Howick Hall*

*Howick Seahouses – The Petrified Forest*

*Silver Sands, Howick*

# CHAPTER SEVEN

# DUNSTANBURGH CASTLE

DUNSTANBURGH CASTLE was one of the key pieces on the chess board where the power plays of English national politics surrounding the Plantagenet dynasty in the Middle Ages were made. The barony of Embleton, of which Dunstanburgh was a minor part, first became involved with these affairs when Simon de Montfort, the great Earl of Leicester, purchased it in the 13th century from its original Norman-Saxon owners, whose grant of ownership had been confirmed by King Henry I. Simon de Montfort soon lost it on his death at the Battle of Evesham, after open rebellion against his brother-in-law King Henry III. Henry III gave most of de Montfort's land, including Embleton, to his own younger son, Edmund, on appointing him Earl of Lancaster. In time it passed to his son, Thomas, who was regarded as one of the most powerful and wealthy figures in Europe, holding at once the Earldoms of Leicester, Lincoln, Lancaster, Salisbury and Derby.

This "over-mighty subject" strengthened and fortified his manor house situated on the site of a former "Burh", a fortified tribal centre of the Angles, in about 1315. There are records of limestone and lead and "sea cole" being transported overland from Newcastle, and some of the masons' marks are similar to those used at Warkworth. The Earl paid the ultimate price for his overweening pride, by being decapitated for treason by his cousin, Edward II, but not before he had tortured and executed the King's favourite, Piers Gaveston, in a most horrible fashion. Following his death, Thomas was canonised by the Church for his "generosity and consideration". Dunstanburgh was inherited by his brother Henry, who being a guardian during the minority of Edward III, was later created the first Duke of Lancaster. On the death of Henry, who left no male issue, his estates were divided between his two daughters Maud and Blanche, the wife of John of Gaunt, 2nd Duke of Lancaster and a son of Edward III, who strengthened and enlarged the fortifications, including the building of a grange within the confines of the castle.

Dunstanburgh was never a residence as Warkworth or Alnwick castles were. It had, first and foremost, a military role, being garrisoned by professional troops and commanded by a Constable. During the Wars of the Roses, the castle was the main Lancastrian fortress in the north. Heavily garrisoned by mercenaries, who held it for Queen Margaret of Anjou, wife of

*Dunstanburgh Castle from Newton-by-the-Sea*

Henry VI, it was finally besieged and taken after her defeat at the battle of Hexham in 1464. The heavy bombardment by cannon to which it was subjected then left it in a ruinous condition, in which it has remained ever since.

After 100 years of royal ownership, it was sold to Sir William Grey, Baron of Wark-on-Tweed; he was afterwards succeeded by his son and heir, created 1st Earl of Tankerville. On his death in 1701 Lord Tankerville, left an only daughter Mary, who married Lord Ossulston, who afterwards became 2nd Earl of Tankerville. The barony and estates, being entailed in the male line, passed to the brother of the 1st Earl. The 2nd Earl contested this and, by mutual arrangement, her Ladyship was allotted the manors of Stamford, Embleton and Dunston. These lands continued in the possession of the family until 1869 when they were sold for the then princely sum of £155,000. During this century, a local farmer is reputed to have cropped the nine acres which are enclosed within the walls of the castle, yielding some 240 bushels of corn and several loads of hay, a case surely of "swords into ploughshares". In Sir Walter Scott's poem *Marmion*, when the nuns of St Hilda voyaged northward along this stretch of the coast, they

*Crossed themselves to hear*
*The whitening breakers sound so near*
*Where boiling through the rocks, they roar*
*On Dunstanburgh's caverned shore.*

*Dunstanburgh Castle from Embleton*

*Dunstanburgh Castle from Craster*

# CHAPTER EIGHT

# CRASTER

CRASTER USED to be a very busy little fishing village. It acted as home base and harbour to a large fleet of cobles (the Northumbrian open boat, based upon the Viking longboat design) which harvested the vast shoals of herring that populated the coastal waters until the middle of this century. These days, only a handful of cobles fish from Craster, and they harvest mostly prawns, crab and lobster inshore, with salmon and sea-trout in season, having to travel much further afield to catch the larger white fish.

Another old industry at Craster was quarrying. As the old village is sited just below the Heugh and, consequently, lies right on top of the Great Whin Sill which runs through Northumberland from Hexhamshire to the Farnes, it was natural to make use of this tremendous natural resource. Most of the local structures were built of this stone, from Craster Tower to the old field walls, and even the harbour wall itself. In the 18th and 19th centuries, boatloads of whinstone setts were transported to London for street paving stones. The huge quarry was owned and worked by the Craster family whose income was greatly supplemented by the sale of whinstone.

The Crasters of Craster are one of the oldest families in Northumberland, claiming ancestry back to Norman, and even Saxon times on the distaff side. The family crest is "a Raven proper", the first Grant of Arms being recorded at a herald's visitation of about 1530. The founder of this family is believed to be one Albert, who was in possession of the manor of Craster around or before 1168. The old tower, which is part of the present mansion house, was built before the year 1415. It is mentioned as the property of Edmund Craster in the list of fortresses of that time and still remains in the hands of the Craster family.

A thriving relic of the great herring industry, which once employed so many Craster people, is the Smoke House where the Robson family still cure their world-famous Craster kippers. These are exported all over the world, from Hong Kong to San Francisco. Whilst most of the herring are no longer caught locally, they are still smoked in old kipper sheds in the age-old tradition using hardwood chippings. Salmon and sea-trout are also smoked by the Robsons, who have a substantial "wet-fish" business and a restaurant in the village as well.

Craster is a Mecca for tourists in the summer, but "The Jolly Fisherman" is still a drinkers' pub, and it serves some of the best crab sandwiches in the district. From Craster, the walks to Dunstanburgh Castle and along the coastal path to Howick cover some spectacular scenery and, out of season, the whole area emits a quiet, peaceful ambience – that is, if you can stand the bitter, easterly, sea-breezes.

*Craster*

# CHAPTER NINE

# BAMBURGH CASTLE

T HE STRETCH of coastal farmland running along the shoreline at Bamburgh is, according to the weather records, one of the areas of lowest rainfall in Britain, averaging 21 to 24 inches per annum. This mild, frost-free climate makes it an ideal habitat for the European grassland birds such as the curlew, which can be seen here at nesting time in the spring, and the lapwing which finds the extensive duneland ideally suited to its breeding habits.

It is no accident that the rock on which the castle of Bamburgh stands, like those of Edinburgh and Warkworth, has been used as a stronghold far back in time. The first recorded mention of the castle site relates to Ebba, a Saxon warlord, who is reputed to have landed in the middle of the sixth century with a fleet of sixty longships. He is believed to have fortified the site with a "hedge" (probably some form of rude stockade) but was defeated and driven off by "Uhrien", the warlike king of the Strathclyde Picts. Certainly, at some date after this, he returned and established his "Burgh" (Bebbanburgh) and from him descended a line of Saxon kings whose territory, over the next three or four centuries, expanded or contracted — according to the tide of fortune — from the Kingdom of Bernicia to the Kingdom of Northumbria, and finally, with the rise of the Norman kings of England, to the Earldom of Northumberland. Bamburgh, therefore, has always been an important, often royal, stronghold, as the borders and fortunes of the two kingdoms of Scotland and England swayed back and forth. The present castle is a comparatively modern restoration. Built substantially of sandstone and flint — from a quarry at North Sunderland, some three miles away — unfortunately it is sited to receive every blast of wind from every point of the compass, hence the constant weathering.

Bamburgh has undergone many assaults and sieges, notably that by William Rufus, successor to the Conqueror, of the Norman Earl of Northumberland Robert de Mowbray in 1095. As part of the siege, he built a *Malvoisin* ("evil neighbour" in Norman French) reputedly on the site of Glororum Farm, so that he could "glower-ower-him". Rufus eventually won and, after he had executed de Mowbray, the castle remained in royal hands (nominally, at least), until James I

*Bamburgh Castle*

granted the ruins and the manors to one Claudius Forster, the illegitimate son of Sir John Forster who had held it for the crown in one form or another for most of the previous century. The Forster family sold the castle in 1704, to repay debts and mortgages accumulated as a result of a dissolute life-style.

The castle came into the hands of the Bishop of Durham, Lord Crew in his own right, who married Dorothy Forster, reputedly a great beauty and daughter of Sir William Forster, in 1699. Lord Crew willed everything on his death – including his possessions at Blanchland – to a charitable trust. He died in 1720, and with the trust's funds, the castle's restoration was started in 1757. One of the trustees, Dr Sharp, Archdeacon of Northumberland, zealously carried out the work, and contributed his own funds to achieve his life's ambition.

The other notable figure in the castle's history appeared at the end of the nineteenth century in the form of the first Lord Armstrong. He purchased the castle, and considerably extended and embellished it, making it a superb compliment to his great country house Cragside, near Rothbury. He also arranged for a branch line to be built from the north-east main railway line to North Sunderland and Seahouses for his own convenience.

There is a curious tale concerning one of the Crew trustees' stone masons at Bamburgh. In 1793, one George Wilson found a large and lethargic toad, which he encarcerated in a tomb-like chamber in the stone wall he was building. In 1809, Wilson, who with some other masons was taking down part of the wall in the course of building a gateway, uncovered the poor toad, still alive but in a torpid condition. Upon recovering animation, the toad is supposed to have made its escape into a pile of rubble.

In this century, Bamburgh has found itself on the tourist route, but is largely unspoilt. It is a favourite venue for producers of films with a medieval flavour, and it is here that Elizabeth Taylor and Richard Burton are believed to have carried on their romance among the dunes whilst filming *Becket*.

*Owls: Winter landscape, Bamburgh to the Cheviot Hills*

SPRING in Northumberland has really arrived when the lapwings return from their winter sojourn and begin to nest. In the days before intensive agriculture changed cereal farming, the "whaups" (so called in northern parts of the country and over the border because of their piercing cry) or "pee-weets" (as they are called south of the Coquet) would nest on the bare, unsown land. Often the hind (horseman), following his pair of horses harrowing the land, would pause in his task and carefully lift the new-laid eggs or the freshly-hatched chicks to one side. Even when driving the early tractors, harrowing or rolling (with no air-conditioned, soundproofed cab to sit in and a radio blotting out nature's sounds) tractormen would see and hear the anxious parent lapwings, swooping and diving to distract them from harming their families.

Sadly, nowadays, the winter-sown corn and the modern grass ley is well grown when the lapwings come to nest in spring and, lacking the bare nesting habitat, they move further afield to the marginal uplands of Northumberland to rear their families. The gorse-covered whinstone ridge just north of Bamburgh, still free from modern farming, remains an ideal area for the "whaup" or "pee-weet" to nest.

Often as they worked in the open fields – at all times of the year and in all weathers – farmworkers would watch kestrels hovering above their prey. After harvest was the most interesting time, when the corn was led into the stackyards and before the ploughs began to blacken the soil. Even now, one can watch the odd kestrel hovering and swooping down upon its hapless prey – usually a fieldmouse but occasionally a young partridge.

OLD NORTHUMBRIAN RIDDLE:

*"What's up when its doon, and doon when its up?"*
Answer:
*"The crest on a pee-weet's heed."*
(It lies sleek on its neck when flying; and rises when on the ground.)

*Bamburgh Castle*

# CHAPTER TEN

# LINDISFARNE &
# THE FARNE ISLANDS

*If, on a rock, by Lindisfarne,*
*St Cuthbert sits, and toils to frame*
*The sea-born beads that bear his name;*

*Marmion*, SIR WALTER SCOTT

THE FARNE Islands comprise two groups of islands – the "Inner" and the "Outer" farnes. Now protected and maintained by the National Trust, they are a breeding ground for over 250,000 sea birds and a colony of seals. The most common birds are the puffins who have a curious nesting habit of burrowing under ground to make a safe haven for their eggs. The Pinnacle's islets of the Inner Farnes are home to an estimated population of around 70,000 Puffins. Eels are a major part of the Puffins' diet and in recent years, due possibly to curtailment of sand eel fishing in the area, there has been something of a population explosion, which is now putting pressure on the habitat. The extra numbers burrowing underground, combined with a series of dry summers, is leading to soil erosion on the tops of these rocky islets.

Artic terns have an aggressive habit of dive-bombing the visitor, often causing alarm and sometimes pain when they strike bare-headed humans with their bills and flapping wings. The roseate tern is a colourful variation on the common tern, easily identified by the pinkish hue of its plumage. Larger sea birds such as herring gulls, black-headed gulls, guillemots and shags are there in profusion, nesting precariously on the craggy rockface. The sound of their cries and stench of their droppings make a forceful assult on the senses.

One of the most attractive birds is the eider duck, or "Cuddy's duck" as it is known locally, generally the most docile of the birds of the Farnes. Their nickname comes from the legend that, during St Cuthbert's periods of retreat to his isolated cell on the outer Farnes, the eider ducks plucked the down from their own breasts to provide the Saint with warm covering, rather like the leaves in *Babes in the Wood.* Until the early part of this century, the islanders used to gather the down to make eiderdowns to supplement their income.

*Lindisfarne Castle with Bamburgh Castle in the distance*

*Lindisfarne Castle*

In times gone by, when sea-going craft travelling up the North Sea coast tended to hug the shore, the Farnes were a graveyard of many vessels, the most famous of these being the *Forfarshire*, wrecked in 1838. The efforts of Grace Darling and her father, the lighthouse keeper on the Farnes, to rescue the crew of this vessel are immortalised in Northumbrian and indeed, national history. In the 1850s, Algernon, 4th Duke of Northumberland – being an ex-naval man – was so concerned at the loss of life and property along these Northumbrian coasts, that he substantially supported the modernisation of the primitive system of lighthouses on Coquet Island and the Farnes. He also supported early lifeboat stations along this turbulent coast, from Tynemouth to Berwick, equipping several with atmospheric barometers, one of which still exists in the Fishing Boat Inn at Boulmer.

The much larger island of Lindisfarne, or Holy Island, to the north counts as one of the Inner Farne islands and is famous for its role in the spread and development of early Christianity in the north as well as being of great strategic value. The early history of Lindisfarne Castle is very obscure; it is only a small fortress but, in its day, it was considered of some importance. Initially enlarged and fortified in the reign of Queen Elizabeth I, it was regarded as part of the responsibility of the Governor of Berwick and had a garrison of 10 or 12 men with artillery. In 1643 it was captured by the Parliamentarian naval captain, Richard Haddock, during the Civil War. It was reactivated during the Napoleonic wars but its cannon were removed in 1819. In the early 20th century, it was purchased and restored by Edward Hudson, a successful magazine proprietor who founded *Country Life*. Hudson employed the great architect of the day, Sir Edwin Lutyens (the architect of Imperial New Delhi), and had the gardens laid out by Lutyens's associate Gertrude Jekyll, the foremost garden designer of the day. The Castle is now owned and maintained by the National Trust and is open to the public.

*Farne Islands*

*The Pinnacles: The Inner Farne Islands*

*The Pinnacles: The Inner Farne Islands*

# CHAPTER ELEVEN

# OLD BEWICK
# & BEWICK MOOR

ONE OF Northumberland's characteristic little churches – Holy Trinity, Old Bewick – lies almost hidden from public view, in a cluster of trees along a deserted lane away from the main road from Eglingham to Chatton. Of very ancient origin – certainly early Saxon – it was reroofed and restored at the instigation and in memory of John Longlands, a farmer and land improver, in 1867. He persuaded the 5th Earl of Tankerville and another local landowner, Addison John Baker-Cresswell, to pay for the work.

The early stonework in some parts of the chapel has the same masons' marks as the capitals in the Norman chapel at Durham Castle that existed before 1105. Some of the stones in its west gable have been identified as pre-Romanesque, reused here, something also found at Chillingham Church.

After the Reformation, the chapel fell into decay, and tradition alleges that General Leslie's Scottish troops fighting for the Parliamentary cause also damaged it during the Civil War. Although restored to some extent in 1695, it lay in ruins in 1850 when Langlands first took an interest in it. The chapel contains a stone effigy of a lady of the 14th century, which is reputed to have been carved by a member of the school of sculptors who were based at Alnwick Abbey and flourished until about 1340.

The first recorded Lord of Bewick Manor was Arkil Morell, Constable of Bamburgh and later Sheriff of Northumberland, who slew Malcolm Canmore, King of Scots, at Alnwick in 1093. Morell, who was a henchman of Robert Mowbray, Earl of Northumberland, rebelled against Henry I, as Mowbray had against William Rufus. On Morell's defeat and the forfeiture of his lands and titles, Henry gave the Manor of Bewick to his wife Queen Maud, who bestowed it on Tynemouth Abbey, a daughter house of St Albans Abbey.

After the Dissolution of the Monasteries, the Collingwood family owned or held leases on Bewick until the Ogle family of Eglingham obtained possession, finally selling the manor and its farms to Addison John Baker-Cresswell who built (or re-built) most of the farms and houses in the district, including the village school at Old Bewick.

*Old Bewick Church*

Bewick Moor has an interesting history. At the western edge of the escarpment is a huge mass of sandstone called the Hanging Crag, which has an ancient prediction attached to it:

*As long as the Hanging Crag shall stand*
*There'll aye be a Ha' (Hall) on Bewick Land*

This is still apt; the Hall family still farm at nearby Bewick Folly.

On the summit of Bewick Hill is a large and perfect specimen of an ancient hill fort – the tribal centre of a long dead race. It is similar in size and type to the earthworks to be found at Greaves Ash in the Cheviot foothills near to Linhope.

Further down the hill is Blaw-wearie, the out-bye hirsel for Old Bewick farm. Near to the old, deserted farmhouse and buildings is a small, almost perfect oppidum, or pre-historic mound. This was investigated by Canon Greenwell in the 19th Century. In the 1970s and 80s, the site was excavated and catalogued by Dr Stan Beckinsall much more thoroughly, with the the benefit of modern science to authenticate his findings. Dr Beckinsall is an authority on the "cup and ring" markings in these parts.

The name "Bewick" is Norman-French for "place of the bees" and is noted as such in the Cartulary of the Abbey of St Albans. Bewick Moor is still a favourite place for local beekeepers to take their hives in August for the heather honey. A Scots guest, staying overnight locally, on being presented with a miniature jar of honey at breakfast, remarked acidly to his host, "I see you keep a bee"!

Just south of Bewick Hill is Harehope Hill on which, near the summit, lies a large, freestone (sandstone) tank. This is reputed to have had connections with St Lazarus and the leper colony at nearby Bolton. It is also said locally to have been used for the distillation of gin in years gone by. This story could have some credence due to the profusion of juniper berries which grow near here. Harehope, or part of it, was the home of one Fergus Storey at the end of the 17th century. Storey was a famous piper and once went to London to play before Queen Anne. He was also a famous glutton and, among older members of the population, a large helping on a plate is still called a "Fargy Storey's Crowdie" (Crowdie being a mixture of oatmeal, scalded with boiling water and eaten with salt and skimmed milk).

The four townships of Old and New Bewick, Harehope and East Lilburn were purchased in 1830 by John Cresswell of Cresswell, who assumed the names of Addison and Baker in accordance with the terms of wills of relatives in 1818 and 1840. His wife noted in her diary that the conveyance of Old and New Bewick, East Lilburn and Harehope, "is on 32 sheets of parchment; there are 25 principles to the transaction, 50 witnesses. The stamp duty to the first sheets £1000, and £1 to every other."

*Bewick  Moor*

*Eglingham Burn*

# CHAPTER TWELVE

# FOOT OF BREAMISH – HEAD OF TILL

*Meet together at Bewick Mill*

BEWICK MILL, north of Old Bewick, is where the fast-flowing hill stream of the Breamish, rushing down from the Cheviots, changes to the slow, sullen, treacherous, river Till, which runs its tortuous course through the rich, southern low-lands of Glendale, before reaching its destination at Tillmouth, where it meets the mighty Tweed.

This delightful strip of private woodland glade is a quite haven for wildlife in the area. In springtime it has a virtual carpet of snowdrops and aconites. The hazel and pussywillow coppice, once valued by fishermen as materials for making their crab and lobster pots, grows wild and unused by mankind, but is an important part of the "food chain" and habitat of the riverbank and woodland creatures.

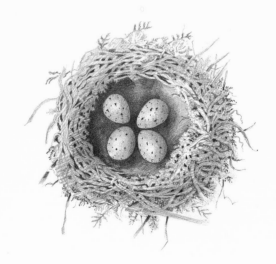

*Foot of Breamish – Head of Till*

# CHAPTER THIRTEEN

# THE RIVER TILL

THE RIVER Till is a slow-moving, meandering stream with deep pools and dangerous currents throughout its length. The bed of the river, coursing along the flat floor of a prehistoric lake, is substantially sand and gravel, but at great depths it overlies deep, thick layers of prehistoric peat. The stream in ages past was notoriously difficult to cross, save at a few fording places which could change in the course of a flood. Until the Middle Ages there were very few bridges. The earliest records show that there were bridges at Doddington when a man accused of theft was captured there in 1310 (Assize rolls), and Tillmouth (circa 1450). Weetwood Bridge is probably the most beautiful bridge over the River Till, three miles east of Wooler. This bridge was constructed in the early part of the 18th century and has survived storms and floods until this day. Only recently — within the last twenty years — has any support work been needed on this structure.

*Weetwood Bridge, River Till*

The bridge at Chillingham Newtown was erected by the 5th Earl of Tankerville in the early part of the 19th Century as an approach to his castle at Chillingham. This Earl also erected a stone bridge between Chatton and Chillingham, and one between Lyham and Henlaw. Two other bridges – one between Fowberry and Hetton House, and one between Hetton House and East Horton – were built largely by the efforts of Matthew Culley, the great farming improver of the early 19th Century, prompted by a tragic drowning, at Fowberry, of a young man crossing the treacherous ford there. The bridge at Ford is generally understood to have been built around the time of the rebuilding of Ford Castle in the late 18th Century. This important bridge also acted as the replacement for an older bridge which used to cross the Till at New Etal. These two bridges, during their time, were important to the coal trade of the area, when pack horses carried panniers of coal to the west and the Scottish border.

Tillmouth, in the 20th century, is more important for its salmon fishing than as an obstacle to marauding Scots, but in its day, the boatmen who ferried passengers across this river just before it reached its final destination at the Tweed, used to be heavily involved in the smuggling trade. Over the centuries, before and after the union of the Crowns and Parliaments, smuggling has always been regarded as a legitimate trade. In the early Middle Ages, horses and salt were the main imports into Scotland, whereas in the 17th and 18th centuries, it was spirits.

The Excise men (or "gaugers" as they were called) used to watch regularly for the prevention of smuggling. On one occasion, two gaugers were in hot pursuit of a notorious smuggler called "Alley Geggy". On coming to the banks of the Till, they hailed the boatman and demanded in the "King's Name" the use of his boat for the pursuit of the smuggler. On jumping into the boat, they did not observe the boatman holding the oar and pushing the boat out into the midst of the fast flowing stream. The boatman, casting aside his disguise, shouted "Ye're awa, an awm Alley Geggy", whereupon the current caught them and took their oarless craft for several miles downstream before they could land.

*Tweed said to Till,*
    *"What gars (makes) ye rin sae still ?"*
*Till said to Tweed,*
    *"Tho ye rin wi' speed,*
*And I rin slow,*
    *Whar ye droon ae man,*
*I droon twa".*

*Chillingham Newtown Bridge*

*Tillmouth*

*The River Tweed at Horncliffe*

*Weetwood Bridge, River Till*

# CHAPTER FOURTEEN

# GLENDALE

THE WHOLE area of the southern part of Glendale, drained and watered by the rivers Till and Breamish, is the bed of a huge prehistoric lake which has left large deposits of sand and gravel. These, mixed with the light sandly soil, can make farming difficult. Whilst rich in minerals, it is also rich in history. On the higher ground are concentrated clusters of man's early dwellings, Iron Age remains, and cup and ring markings on the rocky outcrops; all testifying to mankind's beginnings in this area. Skirmishes and battles between British and Romans, Saxons and Danes, Scots and English, and even British and Germans, have all left their mark; the Cheviots are littered with sites of crashed Allied Airforce planes, as well as German fighters and bombers — grim memorials of the Second World War.

The prehistoric rock markings, known as "Cup and Ring" are one of the great enigmas of Northumberland. They are generally reckoned to be about 4,000 years old, and are believed to be religious symbols used by late neolithic and early bronze age people at a time when farming of a primitive sort was replacing hunting and gathering as a means of sustaining life. These deeply incised carvings are generally to be found on the fell-sandstone rocks which lie on the ridges which carry the ancient complex of routeways over most of the high, bleak moorlands in the north of the county. As their title suggests, the markings take the form of a series of deep, circular cups and associated circles, carved — presumably by stone or flint tools — to form intricate and varied patterns.

CUP AND RING MARKINGS

There is an old Glendale legend that has to do with the "Cushat" (Woodpigeon), which has always been the bane of the farmer's life, especially when it voraciously grazed his clover seeds and his turnip crop. These days, it greedily "scoffs" his oil-seed rape in the late winter and early spring, and gets shot for its pains. The cushat communicates its message by a vigorous "coo-ing" sound; it coos its warning of impending danger; it coos its love-song to its mate. Some people can hear messages in its coo-ing, for instance – "Milk the coo (cow) clean, Kitty!" "Tak twa coos!" – and thereby hangs the tale.

In Glendale many years ago, Tammy took it into his head to steal his neighbour's "coo". As he slunk through the woods on his nefarious escapade, nothing broke the stillness of the night, except for the coo-ing of the cushat. Tammy's neighbour had two cows; Tammy took one and left the other. Driving the "coo" back through the woods, Tammy – who, by this time was congratulating himself at the ease of his conquest – stopped to have a swig or two at his hip-flask. As he drank, his fuddled brain seemed to hear the cushat speaking to him: "Coo-coo-tak-twa-coos-Tammy", the cushat seemed to say. "Coo-coo-tak-twa-coos-Tammy", the Cushat repeated. Tammy thought to him-self, "Why not? – I might as weel be hangit (hanged) for twa coos as yin", so he went back to steal the second cow. Unfortunately, Tammy was caught in the act, and was convicted and hanged. In the end, John Barleycorn – or the cushat – got Tammy hanged.

*Routing Linn*

# CHAPTER FIFTEEN

# LINHOPE SPOUT

LINHOPE SPOUT is the name of a waterfall located at the conjunction of several little hill burns which drain the heather peatlands on the southern flank of Cheviot. It is quite remarkable that the sudden confluence of all these little streamlets can suddenly produce a spectacular waterfall where the peat comes to the edge of the granite rock before tumbling down a little gorge and dene, and eventually joing the river Breamish. This is a very popular spot for walkers who use the various ancient foottracks that criss-cross the Cheviot foothills at the head of the Breamish valley. It is spectacular walking country, with tremendous views right over the east and north of Northumberland.

These hill burns are important corridors for wildlife – small birds, insects and reptiles. The open moorlands are refuge of the red grouse, the hill partridge, hare and, of course, that arch predator, the fox. The adder is the venomous inhabitant of the stone cairns and the river banks, whilst the brown trout basks and flits throughout these sunlit and shaded water courses.

*Linhope Spout*

*Linhope Burn*

*Linhope Burn*

# CHAPTER SIXTEEN

# FAWDON HILLS

*Ther never was a tym on the Marche Partes*
*Sen the Douglas and Percy met,*
*But it was marvele an the rede blude ran not,*
*As the rain does in the Stret.*

*Ancient Border Rhyme*

THE FAWDON Hills at the south-eastern tip of the Cheviots conveniently shelter the Ingram Valley from the bitter south-east winds that scour up from "Howick Hole" in the spring of the year. At this season – around the middle of March until the middle of May – these hills present a barren aspect. It is lambing time and, in pleasant weather, life can be delightful, watching the Brown Hare (Lepus Timidus) perform his courtship dance, the Lapwing swooping and diving, and the Grey Partridge (Perdix Perdix) – there are still a few here – scuttling about after pairing up. This is still grass and stock country, in stark contrast to the rest of Glendale.

Near to Fawdon Farm is the small property known as "The Clinch". This cottage and grazing is the "out-bye hirsel" of the farm. At the begining of the 14th Century, a dispute over ownership – through a marriage settlement – was the cause of the great feud between the Douglas and Percy families, which lasted for centuries. In the middle of the 18th Century, it was the cause of a lawsuit between the then owner, "The Proud" Duke of Somerset (husband of a Percy heiress), and the first Lord Ravensworth, over boundaries. Somerset won, and the land is still in the ownership of the Percys, as it has been since 1309.

A few miles further north, at the northernmost end of those foothills, lies Humbleton Hill, another scene of bloody carnage, where Harry Percy ("Hotspur") and his brother, Ralph, ambushed a Douglas raiding party heading home after a foray. The resultant capture of "The Douglas" by "Hotspur" ultimately led to the rebellion against Henry IV and the battle of Shrewsbury, at which Hotspur lost his life with Sir James Douglas, the captive, fighting for him at his side.

*Fawdon Hills (the Cheviots)*

# CHAPTER SEVENTEEN

# PERCY'S CROSS

THE CONFLICT at Hedgeley Moor occurred on St Mark's day (April 25th) 1464. Lancastrian forces, led by Lords Hungerford and Ros with Sir Ralph Percy and his brother James, attempted to ambush a Yorkist force under Sir John Neville (Lord Montague). Hungerford and Ros fled at the outset, and Sir Ralph Percy received his fatal wound from victorious Yorkist forces.

The battlefield is marked by two monuments of stone, the first being two monoliths of very ancient origin thirty feet apart. They are called "Percy's Leap", and are supposed to mark the distance of Sir Ralph's leap which he made when mortally wounded – a case of legend borrowing from pre-history, as the monoliths pre-date Sir Ralph's time by millenia.

Half a mile to the south of these stones is a stone pedestal of more recent (16th Century) erection, bearing the arms of the Percy and de Lucy families. This stone is sited at the northernmost point of the ancient Percy Barony of Beanley, and is still maintained by the Percy family, although the Beanley Estate is now owned by the Carr-Ellison family of Hedgeley Hall. Near here is also a well – locally called Percy's Well – but marked on one of the old estate maps at Alnwick, as Sir James' Well.

There are some interesting place names in this area, such as the "Cat's Paw" – a bend in the A697 road, now bypassed. The "Play Piece" is an old name for Lilburn Glebe, and in medieval times this was the site of a fair where rural commerce and sports such as footracing, archery and horseracing took place. During a road-widening scheme here in the mid-19th Century, the base of an ancient market cross was uncovered in the form of a sandstone socket which probably held the upright of a timber cross. "The Apron full of Stones" is an interesting and unusual field name on one of the nearby farms, which tells us the nature of the soil.

*Percy Cross with Hedgehope, Cheviot and Roddam Hall in the distance*

# CHAPTER EIGHTEEN

# RODDAM

RODDAM IS the ancient seat of the Roddam family, one of the oldest families in Northumberland, of early Saxon origin. Originally, their charter is said to have been granted by King Athelstan after the battle of Broomridge, the site of which is said to be near Branxton. The legend goes that King Athelstan, victorious on the battlefield, asked for proof of the ownership of the property, whereupon "Pole" (or Paulinus) Roddam produced his sword as his character. At this, Athelstan is reputed to have given him his written charter which, according to the *Scottish Heraldry* is written in Saxon characters as follows:

*I King Athelstan*
  *Giffis heir to Paulane*
*Odam and Roddam*
  *Als gud and Als fair*
*Als ever tha myn ware*
  *And yair to witness Mald my wife.*

Like most old Northumberland families, the Roddams were never rich, but ever faithful and always fighting. Members of the family fought and died in the Border Conflicts, the French Wars, the Civil Wars and, possibly, as a result, lost rather more than they won. In the middle of the 18th Century, the family was described by a north country clergyman in a laconic will who laments that "the proud Roddams like the Delavals who merrily dance in their rags, cannot sell their ancient lineage".

The family fortunes were somewhat restored by Robert Roddam, who went to sea as a young midshipman in 1735-36. With the patronage of Admiral Sir Chaloner Ogle (another Northumbrian ) he quickly rose in the naval service. He inherited his brother's estates in 1776, built the present Roddam Hall and considerably improved and developed his family property. He died in 1808 at 83 years of age, having attained the rank of Admiral of the Red – the highest professional rank in the Royal Navy of that time. The family remained at Roddam until the 1970s.

*The Cheviot Hills*

# CHAPTER NINETEEN

# CUDDY'S CAVE

*Ye were aye stickin in a tree*
*They will be grown while ye're sleepin*

NORTHUMBRIAN LEGEND has it that, as a young boy, St Cuthbert spent his early days working among his father's sheep at Wrangham, on the North Doddington moors. One of the caves which abound in these parts is reputed to have been his sheltering place. This "Cuddy's Cave" lies snugly on the westward edge of the Kyloe Hills, just south of the ancient and tiny village of Holburn. It is approached through Holburn Grange farm, where there is a discreet and convenient car park on the drove road leading to the cave. It is situated within a 10-acre plantation of Scots pines, planted by the late Colonel Gerard Frederick Towlerton Leather (1865-1941), who also had the Bishop of Newcastle consecrate the whole area so it could be used as a family burial plot. Thus this plantation is now doubly holy ground because of its associations with St Cuthbert. The good Colonel lies before the "Bishop's Mitre" (a huge, sandstone rock which lies at the front of the cave), accompanied by the ashes of his son, Mark.

On the top of the rocky outcrop, which is above the cave, the sandstone is very crudely marked. It is believed by some that these marks are associated with the various "Cup and Ring" markings which are quite common in the area. There is also a local legend that the marks were created "when Satan hanged Cuddy's granny in chains out of spite". Some sceptics, however, insist that the marks were caused by weather erosion over the centuries.

The National Trust, who now look after this beautiful and peaceful place, assert on their site plaque that it was merely a resting place for the Saint's remains during their flight from Holy Island to Durham, after the Viking raids in the 10th Century.

*Saint Cuthbert's Cave*

# CHAPTER TWENTY

# COLLEGE VALLEY

COLLEGE VALLEY gets its name from the burn (or stream) which drains the northern side of "Muckle Cheviot" – the cold (or "ca-ad") side of it – and courses in a north-easterly direction to join the river Glen, a tributary of the rivers Till and Tweed.

At the entrance to the valley lies the mansion house of Hethpool, enlarged and ornamented by a former owner, the late Sir Arthur Munro-Sutherland, the great Tyneside industrial and shipping magnate who made his fortune in the earlier part of this century. Formerly, the Grey family held this estate for centuries in the teeth of the marauding Scotts and Kers who lived just over the border in the Bowmont and Kale valleys, at the western end of the estate.

Then the Hethpool and Caldburn properties came into the Collingwood family as part of the dowry of Admiral Lord Collingwood's wife. This veteran of Trafalgar is said to have planted the oak trees growing in the vicinity.

In the 18th and 19th Centuries, this was important sheep farming country and, in the latter half of the 19th Century, the property was farmed by a Miss Reed, a great breeder and improver of the native Cheviot sheep. Quoting Samuel Donkin, the Rothbury auctioneer, who sold up her stock in 1883, "throughout a period of sixty years, the annual drafts of the Hethpool stock have made Hethpool a shibboleth on the Borders".

*College Valley*

In the heart of the College Valley, is the "Cuddystane", near to Southernknowe farm. This is associated with St Cuthbert, but was also the site of a border tryst (or horse fair). The recreation hall for the inhabitants of the valley is to be found at the Cuddystane these days.

The green roads (or drove roads) which criss-cross these uplands were, centuries ago, the haunt of the cattle drovers and the gypsies whose main stock-in-trade were horses of every kind.

This is delightful walking country, with passages to Cheviot and the Pennine Way, past the isolated hill farms of Dunsdale and Goldscleugh on one route, and Mount Hooley and Fleehope on another. The estate, which is private property, has provided a car park at Hethpool and issues permission passes at the Estate Office (Sale & Partners) in Wooler (free of charge to walkers). The valley is home to the famous College Valley Fox Hounds. Started just after the Great War by Sir Alfred Goodson, with the support of neighbouring friends and farmers, this unique pack of hill foxhounds was formed to control the hill fox population in this sheep-farming area before the advent of gas, poison and the snare as a means of pest control. At the right time of year, there is nothing more exhilarating to the Border countryman than the sight and sound of these hounds cresting a ridge in pursuit of their quarry, with the brazen notes of the hunting horn blowing the "Gone Away".

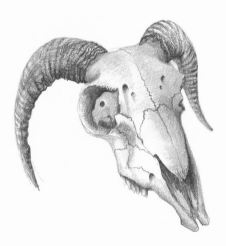

*Cobles at Boulmer*

*Bluebell Wood, Doxford*

# EPILOGUE – THREATS AND SURVIVALS

## BLUEBELLS

THERE ARE now fewer and fewer true Bluebell Woods left in Northumberland. This is largely due to present-day forestry management and practice. The Bluebell appears in early spring, covering the floor of the old hardwood plantations that have been thinned over the years, but not underplanted with young saplings. Often, in this part of the world, after the Bluebells have died back they are followed by a covering blanket of bracken, which shields them from drought and sunlight. Bluebells have one major predator: the human being who digs them up and replants them in his garden.

## THE COBLE

A remarkable little craft, the "Coble" (pronounced "Ceuble" in the Northumberland dialect) has been used for fishing along the coast from Holy Island to Spurn Head for more than a thousand years. It was first mentioned in the Lindisfarne Gospels around 964 A.D. Tradition has it that the Coble is in the direct line of descent from the old Norse longboats which carried the Viking rovers to our shores all those centuries ago. These boats must be strong enough to survive the roughest seas and yet be light enough to be drawn manually up onto the beaches out of harm's way in winter time. Until recently they were being built locally in Harrison's boatyard in Amble.

Boulmer is one of the few unspoilt fishing villages left on the Northumberland coast. A sight still to be seen on an evening is nearly a score of these boats riding at anchor in Boulmer Haven. Not many of them, however, fish commercially these days, although Stevensons and Stantons – old established fishing family names – still live at Boulmer. The fishermen's cottages and the

Manor of Boulmer are still the property of the Percy family, and their bailiff, Geordie Stanton, still presides over their interests from his cottage in the village.

Because of the changes in fishing right along this coast, salmon, sea trout, lobster and crab in season have replaced the herring which once formed the main harvest of the ocean, but there is still cod and other white fish to be caught further out to sea by these sturdy boats manned by sturdy men.